Ida B. Wells

Ida B. Wells
(1862–1931)

QUOTATIONS
OF
Ida B. Wells

APPLEWOOD BOOKS

Biographical information
and quote selection courtesy
of Richard Smith

Cover portrait courtesy of the
National Portrait Gallery

For a complete list of books
currently available, please visit us
at www.applewoodbooks.com

ISBN 978-1-4290-0608-8

Printed in the USA

Ida B. Wells

Ida B. Wells-Barnett was born enslaved in Holly Springs, Mississippi, on July 16, 1862–six months before the Emancipation Proclamation. Ida was the first child of James Madison Wells and Elizabeth "Lizzie" (Warrenton), and the couple had seven more children.

Ida was educated at Rust College in Holly Springs, where her father was a trustee. She dropped out in 1878 after her parents and a sibling died in a yellow fever epidemic, and at the age of sixteen she became a teacher to support her siblings. Her teaching career ended in 1891 when the school board declined to renew her contract due to her criticism of racial injustice.

While riding a train in September 1883, Ida refused to move from the all-white first-class cabin to the smokers' car and was forcibly removed by the conductor. She sued the railroad company for damages, and although she won the initial lawsuit, she lost on appeal. She sued a second time after a similar incident in May 1884, again winning the initial suit, but the verdict was overturned by the Tennessee Supreme Court.

The lynching of three Black men in Memphis in 1892, including close friend

Thomas Moss, spurred Wells to launch an anti-lynching campaign. Her public writings in the *Memphis Free Speech* led to a mob attack on her newspaper office and her subsequent flight from Memphis.

Wells gained notoriety throughout the 1890s as she reported on lynchings across the country. Thanks to her investigative journalism, Wells became a national hero to Black America and was hailed as the "Princess of the Press." She helped found several significant civil rights organizations, including the National Association of Colored Women and the NAACP.

In 1895, Wells married attorney Ferdinand L. Barnett, the owner of *The Conservator*, a weekly Black newspaper in Chicago. Ida served as the editor of the newspaper for two years, but by 1904, with four children and a household to manage, she had stopped contributing magazine and newspaper articles. Wells remained dedicated to social advocacy for the rest of her life, speaking out for women's suffrage and Black political empowerment.

Over an almost forty-year career, Wells wrote countless editorials, columns, reports, pamphlets, and books about racial injustice in America. She died in Chicago on March 25, 1931, at the age of sixty-eight.

Quotations
of
Ida B. Wells

I do not remember when or where I started school. My earliest recollections are of reading the newspaper to my father and an admiring group of his friends... Our job was to go to school and learn all we could.

—*Crusade for Justice: The Autobiography of Ida B. Wells* (1970)

Ida B. Wells.

In a little while [the conductors]... came back and told me I would have to go in the other [railroad train] cars... I refused. The moment he caught hold of my arm I fastened my teeth in the back of his hand. I had braced my feet against the seat in front and was holding to the back, and as he had already been badly bitten he didn't try it again by himself. He went forward and got the baggage man and another man to help him and of course they succeeded in dragging me out.

—*Crusade for Justice: The Autobiography of Ida B. Wells* (1970)

I had formed my ideals on the best of Dickens's stories, Louisa May Alcott's, Mrs. A.D.T. Whitney's, and Charlotte Bronte's books, and Oliver Optic's stories for boys. I had read the Bible and Shakespeare through, but I had never read a Negro book or anything about Negroes.

–*Crusade for Justice: The Autobiography of Ida B. Wells* (1970)

Ida B. Wells

I am not a Democrat, because the Democrats consider me a chattel and... have refused [the Negro] the ballot... and refused him his rights. I am not a Republican, because... they suffered the crimes against the Negro... to go unpunished and almost unnoticed...

–Memphis *Living Way* newspaper, November 7, 1885

O, woman, woman! Thine is a noble heritage!

—New York *Freeman*, December 26, 1885

Preserve me from narrowness and bigotry, I sincerely pray.

—Ida B. Wells Diary, June 15, 1886

Among the many things that have transpired to dishearten the Negroes in their effort to attain a level in the status of civilized races, has been the wholesale contemptuous defamation of their women . . . We only wish to be given the same credit for our virtues that others receive.

—"Our Women," *New York Freeman*, January 1, 1887

God help me to be a Christian! To so conduct myself in my intercourse with the unconverted. Let it be an ever-present theme with me, & O help me to better control my temper!

–Ida B. Wells Diary, January 3, 1887

Ida B. Wells

I am not happy & nothing seems to make me so. I wonder what kind of a creature I will eventually become?

–Ida B. Wells Diary, March 20, 1887

Ida B. Wells

The Negro is the backbone of the South; his labor has cleared the forests, drained the swamps, tilled the soil, built the railroads and dotted the wilderness with cities. He is the preferred laborer of the section of the country and he needs to be taught how to utilize that power for his own benefit.

–Speech at Proceedings of the American Association of Colored Educators, Nashville, Tennessee, December 29th to 31st, 1891

The city of Memphis has demonstrated that neither character nor standing avails the Negro if he dares to protect himself against the white man or become his rival... There is therefore only one thing left to do; save our money and leave a town which will neither protect our lives and property, nor give us a fair trial in the courts, but takes us out and murders us in cold blood when accused by white persons.

—Memphis *Free Speech and Headlight*, 1892

Ida B. Wells

I had bought a pistol the first thing after Tom Moss was lynched, because I expected some cowardly retaliation from the lynchers. I felt that one had better die fighting against injustice than to die like a dog or a rat in a trap.

—*Crusade for Justice: The Autobiography of Ida B. Wells* (1970)

Nobody . . . believes that old threadbare lie that Negro men assault White women. If Southern men are not careful, a conclusion might be reached which will be very damaging to the moral reputation of their women.

—Memphis *Free Speech and Headlight*, May 21, 1892

Ida B. Wells

The realm of fiction yet remains undisturbed by the Afro-Americans as a positive factor in a permanent way. This is much to be regretted, because he occupies so large a position, as a negative force. With slavery for a subject, Mrs. Harriet Beecher Stowe gave America its strongest work of fiction, but the Afro-American there represented, though true in its delineation to the life it represented, does not represent the Afro-American of to-day. Our best literary friends have failed to do it, so ineradicable is prejudice.

—"The Afro-American in Literature," Concord Literary Circle, Concord Baptist Church, Brooklyn, NY, September 15, 1892

The way to right wrongs is to turn the light of truth upon them.

–*Southern Horrors: Lynch Law in All Its Phases* (1892)

Ida B. Wells

Somebody must show that the Afro-American race is more sinned against than sinning, and it seems to have fallen upon me to do so.

–*Southern Horrors: Lynch Law in All Its Phases* (1892)

Ida B. Wells

If labor is withdrawn capital will not remain. The Afro-American is thus the backbone of the South. The white man's dollar is his god, and to stop this will be to stop outrages in many localities.

–*Southern Horrors: Lynch Law in All Its Phases* (1892)

The lesson this teaches and which every Afro-American should ponder well, is that a Winchester rifle should have a place of honor in every black home, and it should be used for that protection which the law refuses to give.

—*Southern Horrors: Lynch Law in All Its Phases* (1892)

Ida B. Wells

Those who commit the murders write the reports.

—*Southern Horrors: Lynch Law in All Its Phases* (1892)

Ida B. Wells

The colored people of this great Republic number eight million... The labor of one half of this country has always been, and is still being done, by them... the wealth created by their industry has afforded to the white people of this country the leisure essential to their great progress in education, art, science, industry, and invention.

—*The Reason Why the Colored American is Not in the World's Columbian Exposition*, 1893

The Negro has as good a right to a fair trial as the white man, and the South will not be free from… horrible crimes of mob law so long as the better class of citizens try to find excuse for recognizing "Judge Lynch."

–*The Reason Why the Colored American is Not in the World's Columbian Exposition*, 1893

If it could be established, a fearlessly edited press is one of the crying necessities of the hour. Such a journal, edited in the midst of such conditions as exist in the South, can better give the facts, than out of it, or than the press dispatches will do.

–"Requirements of Southern Journalism," Speech delivered to the National Press Association and published in the *Zion Church Quarterly*, 1893

The lyncher has become so bold, he has discarded his mask and the secrecy of night, has left the out-of-the-way village and invaded the jails and penitentiaries of our largest cities, and hung and tortured his victims on the public streets.

—"Requirements of Southern Journalism," Speech delivered to the National Press Association and published in the *Zion Church Quarterly*, 1893

Ida B. Wells

If indeed "the pen is mightier than the sword," the time has come as never before that the wielders of the pen belonging to the race which is so tortured and outraged, should take serious thought and purposeful action.

—"Requirements of Southern Journalism," Speech delivered to the National Press Association and published in the *Zion Church Quarterly*, 1893

I see the Memphis *Daily Commercial* pays me the compliment of calling me a "negro adventuress," and violently abuses the English people for listening to me.

—*The Cleveland Gazette*, July 14, 1894

If the South would throw as much energy into an effort to secure justice to the negro as it has expended in preventing him from obtaining it all these years... the problem would soon be solved.

—*The Cleveland Gazette*, July 14, 1894

Our work is only just begun; our race—hereditary bondmen—must strike the blow if they would be free.

—"She Pleads for Her Race: Miss Ida B. Wells Talks About Her Anti-Lynching Campaign," *New York Herald Tribune*, July 30, 1894

The negro is not free, in spite of the Emancipation Proclamation; that noble document has been a dead-letter in the south for the last thirty years.

–"She Pleads for Her Race: Miss Ida B. Wells Talks About Her Anti-Lynching Campaign," *New York Herald Tribune*, July 30, 1894

Ida B. Wells

In the death of Frederick Douglass we lost the greatest man that the Negro race has ever produced on the American continent.

–*Crusade for Justice. The Autobiography of Ida B. Wells* (1970)

The student of American sociology will find the year 1894 marked by a pronounced awakening of the public conscience to a system of anarchy and outlawry which had grown during a series of ten years to be so common, that scenes of unusual brutality failed to have any visible effect upon the humane sentiments of the people of our land.

—*The Red Record: Tabulated Statistics and Alleged Causes of Lynching in the United States* (1895)

Ida B. Wells

The entire system of the judiciary of this country is in the hands of white people. To this add the fact of the inherent prejudice against colored people, and it will be clearly seen that a white jury is certain to find a Negro prisoner guilty if there is the least evidence to warrant such a finding.

—*The Red Record: Tabulated Statistics and Alleged Causes of Lynching in the United States* (1895)

Burning and torture here lasts but a little while, but if I die with a lie on my soul, I shall be tortured forever. I am innocent.

—*The Red Record: Tabulated Statistics and Alleged Causes of Lynching in the United States* (1895)

The matter came up for judicial investigation, but as might have been expected, the white people concluded it was unnecessary to wait the result of the investigation—that it was preferable to hang the accused first and try him afterward.

—*The Red Record: Tabulated Statistics and Alleged Causes of Lynching in the United States* (1895)

We refuse to believe this country, so powerful to defend its citizens abroad, is unable to protect its citizens at home. Italy and China have been indemnified by this government for the lynching of their citizens. We ask that the government do as much for its own.

—Petition to President McKinley,
The Cleveland Gazette, April 9, 1898

Our country's national crime is lynching. It is not the creature of an hour, the sudden outburst of uncontrolled fury, or the unspeakable brutality of an insane mob. It represents the cool, calculating deliberation of intelligent people.

—"Lynch Law in America," speech, Chicago, 1900

Everybody had been quoted on the subject of separate schools except those most vitally concerned—the Negroes.

—Letter to *The Chicago Tribune* on school segregation, 1900

Although lynchings have steadily increased in number and barbarity during the last twenty years, there has been no single effort put forth by the many moral and philanthropic forces of the country to put a stop to this wholesale slaughter. Indeed, the silence and seeming condonation grow more marked as the years go by.

—"Lynch Law in America," speech, Chicago, 1900

When this conscience wakes and speaks out in thunder tones, as it must, it will need facts to use as a weapon against injustice, barbarism and wrong. It is for this reason that I carefully compile, print and send forth these facts.

—*Mob Rule in New Orleans* pamphlet (1900)

Ida B. Wells

In every single instance except one these burnings were witnessed by from two thousand to fifteen thousand people, and no one person in all these crowds throughout the country had the courage to raise his voice and speak out against the awful barbarism of burning human beings to death.

—*Mob Rule in New Orleans* pamphlet (1900)

Men and women of America, are you proud of this record which the Anglo-Saxon race has made for itself? Your silence seems to say that you are. Your silence encourages a continuance of this sort of horror. Only by earnest, active, united endeavor to arouse public sentiment can we hope to put a stop to these demonstrations of American barbarism.

–*Mob Rule in New Orleans* pamphlet (1900)

Ida B. Wells

No good result can come from any investigation which refuses to consider the facts. A conclusion that is based upon a presumption, instead of the best evidence, is unworthy of a moment's consideration.

–"Lynching and the Excuse for It," *The Independent*, May 16, 1901

When President McKinley was assassinated, Theodore Roosevelt became president... Booker T. Washington became his political advisor so far as the colored people in this country were concerned. There were those of us who felt that a man who had no political strength in his own state and who could do nothing whatsoever to elect a president... was not the man to be the advisor as to the political appointment of colored men...

–*Crusade for Justice. The Autobiography of Ida B. Wells* (1970)

We are still reading [*The Souls of Black Folks*] with the same delighted appreciation. I am arranging myself for a meeting of our best brained, to have a discussion thereon, within the next two weeks. I am only sorry that you cannot be present with us.

–Letter to W.E.B. DuBois, May 30, 1903

No human agency can tell how many black diamonds are buried in the black belt of the South, and the opportunities for discovering them become rarer every day as the schools for . . . training become more cramped and no more are being established.

—"Booker T. Washington and His Critics," *The World Today*, April 1904

Ida B. Wells

Mr. Washington says in substance: Give me money to educate the Negro and when he is taught how to work, he will not commit the crime for which lynching is done. Mr. Washington knows when he says this that lynching is not invoked to punish crime but color, and not even industrial education will change that.

—"Booker T. Washington and His Critics," *The World Today*, April 1904

While the country was preparing to celebrate Lincoln's 100th anniversary [in 1909], the Negro race, whose history was inseparably linked with that of Lincoln, was still far from emancipation [with] lynchings, peonage, convict lease systems, disfranchisement, and the Jim Crow cars of the South.

—*Crusade for Justice: The Autobiography of Ida B. Wells* (1970)

We thus launched the movement which now has the national reputation as the NAACP. This movement, which has lasted longer than almost any other movement of its kind in our country, has fallen far short of the expectations of its founders.

—*Crusade for Justice: The Autobiography of Ida B. Wells* (1970)

The social sphere of the Negro woman of the North, while not so restricted as that of her Southern sister, is also affected by caste influences.

—"The Northern Negro Woman's Social and Moral Condition," *Original Rights Magazine*, April 1910

Ida B. Wells

With no sacredness of the ballot there can be no sacredness of human life itself. For if the strong can take the weak man's ballot when it suits his purpose to do so, he will take his life also.

—"How Enfranchisement Stops Lynchings," *Original Rights Magazine*, June, 1910

Ida B. Wells

I'd rather go down in history as one lone Negro who dared to tell the government that it had done a dastardly thing than to save my skin by taking back what I have said.

—*Crusade for Justice: The Autobiography of Ida B. Wells* (1970)

Either I will go with you or not at all... I am not taking this stand because I personally wish for recognition. I am doing it for the future benefit of my whole race.

–Response to the racial segregation of the Woman's March in Washington, January 1913

Ida B. Wells

Birth of A Nation...was an outrage which ought never to have been perpetrated, nor allowed to be shown here.

–*Crusade for Justice: The Autobiography of Ida B. Wells* (1970)

Ida B. Wells

Public sentiment which has encouraged lynchings by silence or by sensational newspaper accounts must be aroused to see the evil to the whole American Nation. It is an awful commentary on our country's brand of Democracy.

–*The East St. Louis Massacre: The Greatest Outrage of The Century* (1917)

The American thinking public cannot bring back the dead but it can open the prison doors and let these poor defenseless men go free. There must be enough justice in Arkansas to never rest until this great wrong is righted. Not until this is done and the peonage system ended can Arkansas take her place among the brave and the free.

–*The Arkansas Race Riot* (1920)

Hundreds of [black farmers in Arkansas] today are penniless... More than a hundred were killed by white mobs, for which not one white man has been arrested. Seventy-five men are serving life sentences in the penitentiary, and twelve men are sentenced to die. If this is democracy, what is Bolshevism?

–*The Arkansas Race Riot* (1920)

Whenever I think of my dear girls, which is all the time, such a feeling of confidence comes over me. I know my girls are true to me, to themselves and their God wherever they are, and my heart is content.

–Letter to daughters Ida and Alfreda, October 30, 1920

Ida B. Wells

I have had many troubles and much disappointment in life, but I feel that in you I have an abiding joy. I feel that whatever others may do my girls are now and will be shining examples of noble true womanhood.

–Letter to daughters Ida and Alfreda, October 30, 1920

Eternal vigilance is the price of liberty, and it does seem to me that notwithstanding all these social agencies and activities there is not that vigilance which should be exercised in the preservation of our rights.

–*Crusade for Justice: The Autobiography of Ida B. Wells* (1970)

Ida B. Wells

The more I studied the situation, the more I was convinced that the Southerner had never gotten over his resentment that the Negro was no longer his plaything, his servant, and his source of income.

–*Crusade for Justice: The Autobiography of Ida B. Wells* (1970)

Ida B. Wells